Elf-help for Healing from Abuse

GW00467929

Foreword

If you have been abused at any time in your life, you may have asked, "Why me? What did I do to deserve this?" It is a question that many victims of abuse struggle with, as they try to make sense of their experience.

The most important thing to know is that there is nothing you ever could have done to deserve being abused. Though it may take time for you to believe this is true, letting this truth sink in, even a little at a time, will be a key part of your healing journey.

I hope that this booklet will be helpful as you embark on your quest toward healing. In it, you will discover information about the experience and impact of abuse, some thoughts to aid your healing process, reflections on prayer and the life of faith in light of abuse, as well as some signs of healing that will let you know that you are on your way toward living more fully.

Since the path toward healing is rarely straight and smooth, you may sometimes feel that you take one step forward and two steps back. Healing takes time, so be gentle with yourself.

Remember, above all, that you are not alone. Many people who have experienced abuse are on a journey toward healing. Listen to their wisdom and share your own. Trust that the time will come when you no longer are a victim of abuse, but a survivor.

1.

The aim of all abusive behavior
is to gain power and control.
The person who abused you
misused his or her power.
Now, you can choose to use
your power for healing.

2.

While you were being abused, you were robbed of control by the person who abused you, but now you are in control of your future and the pace of your healing.

3.

There is no adequate
explanation for the way you
were treated by the person
who abused you. Try not to
waste too much time and
energy attempting to figure
out why you were abused.
Instead, focus your energy
on healing.

4.

If you were abused as a child, the chances are good that the person who abused you was someone you knew and trusted. He or she may have made you feel so special that you enjoyed the attention. This is a common experience among survivors of childhood abuse and there is no reason to feel ashamed.

5.

Though your abusive situation
was unique, there are
experiences that are shared by
many people who have survived
abuse. Learn as much as you
can from the experiences of
other abuse survivors in order
to better understand your own.

6.

Being abused is an isolating experience. You are not alone now. Find an agency or counselor that specializes in working with survivors of abuse. They will provide resources to aid your healing.

7.

Each of us wears many hats; we are sisters, spouses, parents, and friends. If "survivor of abuse" seems to be the only hat you are wearing, remember that it is just one among many.

8.

Not all abuse leaves bruises, but most abuse leaves scars. Just as physical scars fade but never completely go away, the emotional scars of abuse will always be with you. But the reality that you were abused need not define you.

9.

As you begin the process of
healing, remember: Healing
is a journey, not a destination.

Deep
Woods

10.

There is no single map of your path toward healing because everybody's journey is unique. Trust that you will be given enough light to see your next step along the way.

11.

The first healing step for many survivors is telling the story of their abuse to someone they trust. Keep in mind, though, that the story of your abuse is yours to tell—or not. Yet, silence is an abuser's greatest ally. Telling someone you trust about what happened to you will diminish the abuser's power over you.

12.

If you decide to talk about your experiences, you have the freedom to be selective about what and whom to tell.

13.

As you begin the healing process, you may find that particular smells, places, sounds, and sights trigger painful feelings and vivid memories of the abuse. Learn what your triggers are and discover ways to calm yourself.

14.

Create a plan for calming yourself and use it when you are anxious. You might take a long bubble bath, watch a movie, call a friend, write in your journal, walk through a park, or cuddle with your cat.

15.

The healing process sometimes can be consuming, but make time to focus on other things and think other thoughts. Remember to play!

16.

As you reflect on your abuse experience, your feelings may be conflicted, confusing, and overwhelming. You may sometimes feel like you are going crazy. Feeling crazy and being crazy are not the same things.

17.

You may have an assortment of feelings about your experience and the person who abused you, about the other people in your life, and even God. Let yourself feel all your feelings.

18.

Feelings are not right or wrong. Feelings just <u>are</u>. The important thing is not that you experience certain feelings, but how you respond to them. Strong feelings might sometimes feel overwhelming, but you are in charge of your feelings.

19.

Try saying, I _feel_ sad rather than I _am_ sad, as a reminder that you are more than your feelings. Your feelings do not define you.

20.

Discover ways to express
your feelings in healthy ways.
Sing, hammer nails, garden,
or exercise. Emotions can be
energizing. Expend your
energy creatively.

21.

If you find that the intensity of your feelings interferes with your ability to function through the day, you might consult a counselor who has experience working with survivors of abuse.

22.

In your process of healing, there
will be times when you become
frustrated because the same
issues resurface time after time.
Imagine that you are driving
up a winding mountain road.
Though you circle the mountain
many times, you are in different
places on the journey.

23.

The effects of abuse ripple into many aspects of life, including relationships. For instance, because the person who abused you betrayed your trust, you might hesitate to trust others. Consider joining a support group or working with a therapist to help you navigate new relationships.

24.

If you grew up in an abusive household, you are more likely to become involved with an abusive partner. Learn about the kinds of behavior that may signal a potentially abusive relationship. Be attentive to these "red flags."

25.

You may wonder how much to share about your experience with new people in your life. Pay attention to your motives for wanting to tell your story and trust yourself to know when someone can be entrusted with it.

26.

Experiencing abuse may affect many relationships, including your relationship with God. You might find it hard to pray as you once did. Experiment with new ways of praying. Walk a labyrinth, dance your prayers, even shake your fist at God. Talking with a clergyperson or spiritual director about your faith questions can also help.

27.

If the person who abused you was male, you may find it difficult to envision God as masculine. Explore the wide array of God-images found in the Bible. Have you ever imagined God as a mother hen gathering her chicks, as living water, as a woman searching for a lost coin, or as a rock?

28.

You may feel pressured to forgive the person who abused you, but the decision about whether or not to forgive him or her is yours alone.

29.

Forgiveness is a process rather than an event. Forgiveness is likely to be a later phase of your healing journey rather than the first step. Trust yourself to know when, or if, to begin.

30.

Forgiveness means letting go
of the desire to retaliate against
the person who abused you.
Yet, forgiveness may also
involve holding the person who
abused you accountable for
having harmed you. Seeking
justice and retaliating are not
the same things.

31.

Choosing to forgive the person who abused you does not mean that he or she will be part of your life, nor does it suggest that you must forget the harm that was done to you. Even if you decide to forgive, it is important to remember and learn from your experience.

32.

God created you to be amazingly resilient. Your body and spirit withstood terrible trauma. Your survival is an achievement.

33.

As you look back, remember
that abuse was not God's
plan for you. As you look
ahead, trust that God's grace
will cultivate new life in
you—even from the ashes
of this devastating experience.

34.

Your experience of suffering
may deepen your compassion
for others who are hurting.

35.

You may discover that colors appear brighter, jokes seem funnier, and you step more lightly on the earth.

36.

As the burden of your experience gradually dissipates, you will have more energy. Use it creatively!

37.

You will discover one of life's mysteries: When we choose to face our pain rather than hide from it, we become strong.

38.

One day you will realize that you no longer think of yourself as a victim of abuse. When you have done the hard work of healing, you will find that you have more than survived your experience—you have become more alive!

Rev. Cynthia Geisen has worked in ministry for over 20 years. She currently works as an advocate with survivors of domestic and sexual violence.

Illustrator for the Abbey Press Elf-help Books, **R.W. Alley**, also illustrates and writes children's books, including *Making a Boring Day Better—A Kid's Guide to Battling the Blahs*, a recent Elf-help Book for Kids.

The Story of the Abbey Press Elves

The engaging figures that populate the Abbey Press "elf-help" line of publications and products first appeared in 1987 on the pages of a small self-help book called *Be-good-to-yourself Therapy*. Shaped by the publishing staff's vision and defined in R.W. Alley's inventive illustrations, they lived out the author's gentle, self-nurturing advice with charm, poignancy, and humor.

Reader response was so enthusiastic that more Elf-help Books were soon under way, a still-growing series that has inspired a line of related gift products.

The especially endearing character featured in the early books—sporting a cap with a mood-changing candle in its peak—has since been joined by a spirited female elf with flowers in her hair.

These two exuberant, sensitive, resourceful, kindhearted, lovable sprites, along with their lively elfin community, reveal what's truly important as they offer messages of joy and wonder, playfulness and co-creation, wholeness and serenity, the miracle of life and the mystery of God's love.

With wisdom and whimsy, these little creatures with long noses demonstrate the elf-help way to a rich and fulfilling life.

Elf-help Books

...adding "a little character" and a lot
of help to self-help reading!

Elf-help for Healing from Abuse	#20356
Elf-help for the Mother-to-Be	#20354
Believe-in-yourself Therapy	#20351
Grieving at Christmastime	#20052
Elf-help for Giving the Gift of You!	#20054
Grief Therapy (new, revised edition)	#20178
Healing Thoughts for Troubled Hearts	#20058
Take Charge of Your Eating	#20064
Elf-help for Coping With Pain	#20074
Elf-help for Dealing with Difficult People	#20076
Loneliness Therapy	#20078
Elf-help for Healing from Divorce	#20082
Music Therapy	#20083
'Tis a Blessing to Be Irish	#20088
Getting Older, Growing Wiser	#20089
Worry Therapy	#20093

Book price is $4.95 unless otherwise noted.
Available at your favorite gift shop or bookstore—
or directly from One Caring Place, Abbey Press
Publications, St. Meinrad, IN 47577.
Or call 1-800-325-2511.
www.carenotes.com